EMPLOYIN(WITH DISABILITIES

Michael Evans is a graduate of the Chartered Institute of Personnel and Development and spent several years as a specialist in the field of recruitment and selection. He has been manager of the Employment Disability Unit of Dundee City, Angus Council, and Perth and Kinross Council since 1993 and chairperson of the Scottish Union of Supported Employment since 1997. He now has considerable experience of supporting people with disabilities into employment and of delivering a wide range of services to disabled people, employers and carers.

The Employment Disability Unit has been at the cutting edge of developing UK Government policy by piloting the New Deal for Disabled People and Supported Employment Programmes. Evans also plays a key role within the European Union of Supported Employment and has led training seminars in Estonia, Italy, Sweden and Norway. In March 2001 he organised a three-day international conference on supported employment in Edinburgh, which was attended by 600 delegates from 30 countries.

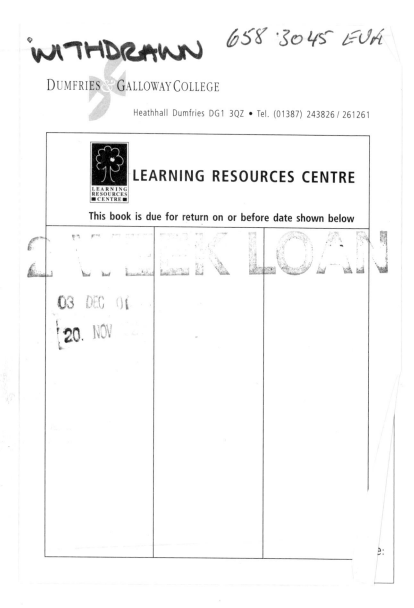

EMPLOYING PEOPLE WITH DISABILITIES

MICHAEL J. EVANS

CHARTERED INSTITUTE OF PERSONNEL AND DEVELOPMENT

First published in 2001

Design and typesetting by
Wyvern 21 Ltd, Bristol

Printed in Great Britain by
the Short Run Press, Exeter

British Library Cataloguing-in-Publication Data
A catalogue record for this book is available
from the British Library

ISBN 0-85292-900-5

Chartered Institute of Personnel and Development, CIPD House, Camp Road, Wimbledon, London SW19 4UX
Tel: 020-8971-9000   Fax:020-8263-3333
E-mail: cipd@cipd.co.uk
Website: www.cipd.co.uk
Incorporated by Royal Charter. Registered charity no. 1079797.

Contents

Disclaimer

The law in this area is changing all the time, and you are advised to seek the advice of a qualified lawyer. Neither the author nor the publisher of this book makes any guarantees or warranties regarding the use of the content of this book.

Other titles in the series

FOREWORD

This book was written by Michael Evans of the Employment Disability Unit of Dundee City, Angus Council, and Perth and Kinross Council in partnership with Michelle Hegarty and Tanya Gilchrist of Capability Scotland. The authors have drawn throughout on their wide experience of dealing with the Disability Discrimination Act (DDA) and of supporting employers and disabled people with employment and training opportunities.

The Employment Disability Unit creates employment opportunities for disabled people and assists people to find and maintain work. The Unit has won many awards, including the European Commission in Scotland Equality Award for the Promotion of Equality for People with Disabilities, and a Convention of Scottish Local Authorities (COSLA) Award for providing the best Quality of Service for a Local Authority Project in Scotland.

Tanya Gilchrist is head of Capability Scotland's Employment Development Department, responsible for the provision of a variety of services to over 300 people with disabilities throughout Scotland. She has worked for Capability Scotland since 1988 and has been instrumental in achieving substantial growth and development of services throughout the country. Her team operates one of the largest Supported Employment Contracts in Scotland and provides national coverage for the Work Preparation Programme. Capability Scotland and the Employment Disability Unit were the two Scottish providers awarded the contract to operate a Supported Employment Initiative designed to influence Supported Employment providers throughout the UK.

Michelle Hegarty studied law at Queen's University Belfast, later graduating with distinction from the MSc programme in public relations at Stirling University in 1993. Now director of communications at Capability Scotland, she has experience of campaigning and of introducing initiatives to influence employers' awareness of the Disability Discrimination Act and attitudes to disability across a wide variety of sectors.

Certain sections of this book have been checked and improved by other professionals whom the authors consider experts in their fields. Many thanks are due to Robyn McIlroy, formerly an employment law specialist with Morison Bishop Solicitors, Scotland, for her help with Chapter 1. The authors would also like to express their gratitude to the Bank of Scotland, and in particular Andy McCarle, for their financial assistance and encouragement in producing this book. This partnership between Capability Scotland, the Employment Disability Unit and the Bank of Scotland offers a prime example of voluntary, public- and private-sector organisations working together to provide equality of opportunities for people with disabilities.

CAPABILITY
SCOTLAND
TURNING DISABILITY
INTO ABILITY

INTRODUCTION

The Disability Discrimination Act 1995 (DDA) gives new rights to employees who are (or become) disabled and places new duties on employers throughout the UK. Hence it is obviously prudent for employers to be aware of this legislation (set out in Chapter 1) and to take steps to meet their obligations.

Yet the fundamental aim of this book is not just to help organisations respect the letter of the law. It always makes business sense to employ the best person for the job and to retain effective staff, regardless of whether they are able-bodied or disabled. Because this is also socially desirable, there is a range of financial and other support available through Government programmes (summarised in Chapter 2). Employers seeking guidance and sources of further help will find here everything they need.

They will also find reassurance on any concerns about the 'reasonable adjustments' they are now required to make to workplace environments and employment processes in order to ensure equal opportunities. Although the law may sound demanding in the abstract, it seldom presents major difficulties to employers who tackle its requirements in a spirit of good will and common sense (see Chapter 5).

The same applies to the advice on 'disability etiquette' that appears in Chapter 4. Although it can never make sense to alienate or offend employees, applicants and customers, gaffes can easily be avoided by anyone who learns the basic rules about sensitive behaviour and appropriate vocabulary.

Together with sound policies on recruitment and retention (see Chapter 3), attention to such issues can make a real difference to the working lives of people with disabilities. It also helps to ensure that employers get and keep the best staff – judged on *ability*, as business effectiveness requires. All organisations in the private, public and voluntary sectors now need to manage diverse workforces. *Employing People with Disabilities* provides a mixture of legal detail, best practice, and information on access and adjustments that will instantly streamline this essential task.

The Disability Discrimination Act 1995 (DDA)

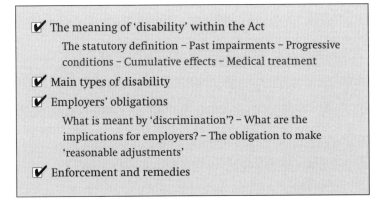

✔ The meaning of 'disability' within the Act

The statutory definition – Past impairments – Progressive conditions – Cumulative effects – Medical treatment

✔ Main types of disability

✔ Employers' obligations

What is meant by 'discrimination'? – What are the implications for employers? – The obligation to make 'reasonable adjustments'

✔ Enforcement and remedies

The DDA legislates for a range of areas such as employment, access to goods, facilities and services, and buying or renting property and land. It came into effect on 2 December 1996 and, although certain provisions of the Act are being phased in over time, the employment provisions came into force on that date. The employment provisions now apply to all businesses employing at least 15 employees.

The meaning of 'disability' within the Act

The statutory definition

The definition of 'disability' in the Act is the same for all the provisions in relation to employment, access to goods, facilities and services, and buying or renting property and land.

Section 1 of the DDA defines a 'disabled' person as 'Anyone with a physical or mental impairment which has a substantial and long-term adverse effect upon their ability to carry out normal day-to-day activities'. The key features in this definition are these:

1 There must be a physical or mental impairment.
2 The impairment must adversely effect the person's ability to carry out 'normal day-to-day activities' such as his or her mobility; manual dexterity; physical co-ordination; continence; ability to lift, carry or otherwise move everyday objects; speech, hearing or eyesight; memory or ability to concentrate, learn or understand; or perception of physical danger.
3 The adverse effect must be 'substantial' (ie not minor).
4 The adverse effect must be 'long term' – that is, to have lasted, or be expected to last, 12 months or more.

Past impairments

A person who had but no longer has a disability will continue to have protection under the definition of 'disabled' within the meaning of the Act.

Progressive conditions

- A person who has a progressive condition is deemed to fall within the description of 'disabled' if he or she has a progressive condition such as cancer, multiple sclerosis, HIV etc.
- The condition must result in an impairment that *has* or *had* an effect upon the person's ability to carry out normal day-to-day activities.
- The condition must result in an impairment that has a substantial adverse effect upon the person's ability to carry out normal day-to-day activities *in the future*.

Cumulative effects

A person may have a number of impairments, none of which alone would have a substantial adverse effect upon the ability to carry out normal day-to-day activities but which, taken together, have a cumulative effect. In such cases account would be taken of whether the impairments together would have such a substantial effect.

Medical treatment

If an employee is taking prescribed medication, and *but for* that medication would have an impairment that would have a substantial adverse effect upon the ability to carry out normal day-to-day activities, then he or she will be deemed to fall within the definition of 'disabled'. (However, correction of eyesight is an exception.)

Main types of disability

No two people who are disabled are the same. Disability affects different people in different ways, but here are some terms that you may hear used to describe such broad types of disability as:

- physical disability: an impairment to the body that affects a person's ability to carry out day-to-day activities
- learning disability: a life-long condition resulting in difficulty in learning or behavioural problems, or both
- mental impairment: the Act says that only those mental impairments that are clinically well-recognised mental illnesses fall within the definition of mental impairment; a mental illness may be temporary or recurring and treatable, and should not be confused with a learning disability
- deafblindness: an impairment of both hearing and sight
- deafness: hearing loss and hearing disorders
- blindness/visual impairment: partial or total loss of sight
- epilepsy: tendency to have recurrent seizures which originate in the brain
- multiple sclerosis: a neurological condition that results from damage to the central nervous system
- ME (myalgic encephalomyelitis), also known as chronic fatigue syndrome or post viral syndrome
- autism: a developmental disorder that affects communication skills
- acquired disability: an impairment that does not

4

occur at birth but at any other stage in life, for example through an accident (such as acquired brain injury).

It is important to remember that there are many other categories of impairment: this list is not exhaustive.

Employers' obligations

The Act makes it unlawful for employers to discriminate against current or prospective disabled employees because of a reason relating to their disability.

What is meant by 'discrimination'?

Discrimination occurs where a disabled person is treated less favourably than someone else and:

- the treatment is given for a *reason relating to the person's disability* and that reason does not apply to the other person
- the treatment *cannot be justified*.

(The Act says that less favourable treatment of a disabled person will be justified only if the reason is both *material* to the circumstances and *substantial*.)

What are the implications for employers?

Employers must not discriminate against a disabled person in relation to:

- recruitment
- the selection process
- terms and conditions of employment
- opportunities for promotion, training or transfer

- employment benefits
- dismissal or any other detrimental treatment.

Recruitment

Employers must ensure that the methods they use to attract potential candidates are not discriminatory against disabled people.

Selection process

It is unlawful to discriminate against a disabled person who is an applicant for employment during any part of the selection process. (This is dealt with more fully in Chapter 3.)

Terms and conditions of employment

An employer may not offer a disabled applicant terms of employment different from or less favourable than those offered to a non-disabled applicant for a reason relating to the applicant's disability.

Opportunities for promotion, training or transfer

Although there is no onus on employers to offer promotion, training or transfer, the law is infringed if discrimination plays a part in the selection process in relation to opportunities for promotion, training or transfer that the disabled person has applied for.

Employment benefits

A disabled person should not be denied any significant benefits that are available to non-disabled employees as part of their employment.

Dismissal or any other detrimental treatment

It is potentially unlawful discrimination if a disabled employee is dismissed for a reason relating to his or her disability. An employee so dismissed requires no qualifying period of employment to make a claim under the DDA.

Employers should therefore be careful when considering dismissal of employees due to long-term ill-health, because that may amount to unlawful discrimination.

In relation to redundancy, employers should be careful that the selection criteria do not discriminate against any disabled employees.

The obligation to make 'reasonable adjustments'

Employers must make 'reasonable adjustments' to their workplace environment and the employment process to ensure that disabled persons are not discriminated against and that they may enjoy equal employment opportunities with others.

The duty upon an employer to make 'reasonable adjust-ments' arises where any arrangements made by, or on behalf of, an employer, or any physical features of premises occupied by the employer, place the disabled person con-cerned at a substantial disadvantage in comparison with persons who are not disabled. It is the duty of the employer to take such steps as are reasonable in order to prevent the *arrangement* or *physical feature* having that effect.

Arrangements

The Code of Practice for the elimination of discrimination in the field of employment (DfEE 1996) gives examples of 'arrangements' that may trigger a duty to make reasonable adjustments, eg:

- arrangements for determining to whom employment may be offered

- any term, condition or other arrangement by which employment, promotion, transfer, training or any other benefit is offered.

Examples of arrangements that could cause disadvantages to disabled people are:

- a starting or finishing time that creates difficulty for someone with a mobility problem
- communication methods and instructions too difficult to understand by a person with a learning disability
- interviews for people with hearing impairments conducted without communicators/signers
- selection/written tests for people with visual impairments.

Physical features

'Physical features' of premises means any that are temporary or permanent, such as:

- any feature arising from the design or construction of a building on the premises
- any feature on the premises or any approaches, or access, to such a building
- any fixtures, fittings, furnishings or furniture equipment in, or on, the premises.

Required changes to physical features may include:

- provision of appropriate toilet facilities
- widening the doors for wheelchair access
- electronic opening doors

- Braille strips on elevator panels
- dropping kerbs on the approaches to buildings
- making available a parking space for a disabled person's car
- altering lighting and appropriate use of colour for people with impaired vision
- ensuring enlarged signs are available for people with impaired vision
- arranging for sink taps to be changed to make them easier to turn on and off by someone with arthritis.

When is it 'reasonable' to make an adjustment?

The employer has a duty to make reasonable adjustments to remove barriers and physical features that cause a disadvantage to a disabled person. The duty upon the employer is only to take such steps as are 'reasonable' within all the circumstances of the case in order to prevent the arrangements or features placing the disabled person concerned at a substantial disadvantage in comparison with a non-disabled person.

Taking relevant circumstances into account

The employer is entitled to take into account all circumstances when deciding what steps it would be reasonable to take, including determining *whether* it is reasonable to have to take a practical step in order to comply with the duty to make reasonable adjustments. Regard should be paid to the following, which are deemed to be considerations:

- the extent to which taking the step would prevent the disabled person from being placed at a substantial disadvantage

- the extent to which it is practical for the employer to take the step
- the financial or other costs that would be incurred by the employer in taking the step
- the extent to which taking the step would disrupt any of the employers' activities
- the employer's financial and other resources
- the availability of any financial or other assistance to take the step.

Reasonable adjustments

The following examples are the kind of reasonable adjustments that an employer may have a duty to make to the workplace environment and employment process in relation to a disabled person:

- adapting the premises
- allocating some of the disabled person's duties to another person
- transferring the disabled person to an existing and more appropriate vacancy
- altering a disabled person's working hours if necessary
- assigning the disabled person to a different place of work
- allowing the disabled person to be absent during working hours for rehabilitation, assessment or treatment
- giving the disabled person training
- acquiring new or modifying existing equipment
- using appropriate methods of communication, instruction or reference manuals
- modifying procedures for testing or assessment

- providing a reader or interpreter
- providing appropriate supervision
- seeking external advice from a service provider such as the Employment Disability Unit or Disability Services Team (see Chapter 6 for useful contacts).

Again, this list is not exhaustive: there are many other examples of reasonable adjustments that could be made.

Enforcement and remedies

Where any employee or prospective employee who is 'disabled' within the meaning of the DDA considers that he or she has been treated less favourably on account of disability then, regardless of the individual's length of employment, he or she can make a complaint of unlawful discrimination to an employment tribunal within three months of the date of the action complained of.

Employment tribunals have powers to:

- make (unlimited) awards of compensation
- make a declaration regarding the rights of the complainant and the respondent in relation to the complaint
- make a recommendation to the employer to take reasonable steps to correct the adverse effect.

Employers should always remember that they are liable for the actions of their employees. For the purposes of the Act, any discriminatory action taken by an employee in the course of his or her employment will be treated as if it was the employer who had taken the action.

Employment programmes and support services

☑ Access to Work Scheme
☑ Workstep (Supported Employment Programme)
☑ Job Introduction Scheme
☑ Support services

A range of financial assistance and support is available to employers who wish to recruit or retain in employment a person with a disability. This support is available from the Government through the Access to Work Scheme, Workstep (the Supported Employment Programme) and other locally based initiatives or projects.

Access to Work Scheme

The Access to Work Scheme offers employers equipment, support or assistance towards any adjustments or adaptations the disabled employee requires in order to do his or her job. The Scheme is run by the Employment Service, which authorises all expenditure.

The type of assistance that can be given to an employer or a disabled person, or both, includes:

13

- provision of a communicator or signer
- provision of a part-time reader or assistant for employees with a visual impairment
- adaptations to existing or new equipment to meet the disabled employee's needs
- alterations to premises or a working environment
- provision of a support worker/job coach for an employee who needs physical help either at work or getting to work
- assistance towards taxi fares if a disabled employee cannot use public transport to get to work.

It is usual for the employer to pay for support and then claim back the grant from the Employment Service's Access to Work Programme.

Access to Work pays a percentage of the total cost of approved support, depending on how long a person has been in employment and what support is needed. For example, Access to Work pays 100 per of the approved costs for:

- previously unemployed people starting a job
- all self-employed people
- people working for an employer who have been in the job for less than six weeks.

Whatever the employment status of the applicant, Access to Work pays 100 per cent of the approved costs of help with:

- support workers
- fares to work
- communicator support at interview.

To people working for an employer who have been in the

job for six weeks or more and who need special equipment or adaptations to premises, Access to Work pays a proportion of the costs of support as follows:

- All support under £300 is to be borne by the employer.
- If the costs involved are between £300 and £10,000, the Employment Service will pay up to 80 per cent.
- If costs exceed £10,000, the Employment Service will pay up to 80 per cent of the costs between £300 and £10,000 and 100 per cent of costs over £10,000.

All help is for a maximum period of three years, after which the Employment Service reviews the individual's circumstances. Access to Work may provide help for a further period if the employee continues to be eligible for help under the rules that then apply.

The Access to Work Scheme can be authorised and approved only by the Employment Service, and there are eligibility criteria for the provision of assistance through this Scheme. For more information on the Access to Work Scheme, contact the Employment Service's Disability Service Team listed in Chapter 6.

Workstep (Supported Employment Programme)

Workstep (the Supported Employment Programme) enables an employer to receive a variety of support to take into account the possibility that an employee with a disability may not be able to undertake the full range of tasks or may have a lower output than other colleagues. (The Supported Employment Programme was renamed Workstep on 1 April 2001.)

Workstep is funded by the Employment Service and operated through contractors or sponsors. The main sponsoring organisations are :

- local authorities (eg Dundee City Council)
- voluntary organisations (eg Capability Scotland)
- Remploy (Britain's largest employer of people with disabilities)

The eligibility of a disabled person to Workstep can be authorised only by the Employment Service. With effect from April 2001 the eligibility criteria are:

- people with a disability on Job Seeker's Allowance for 12 months or more
- people on Incapacity Benefit
- former Supported Employment employees who lose their jobs in mainstream employment within two years of leaving the Programme
- those currently in work but at serious risk of losing their jobs as a result of disability, even after the employer has made all reasonable adjustments.

The Programme can offer a range of support to employers and employees, such as financial assistance or a wage subsidy to the employer, or a job coach/support worker to help the person with a disability settle into the workplace.

The Programme can also provide support to enable eligible individuals to retain their jobs if they would otherwise be unable to continue work owing, for example, to the onset or deterioration of a disability.

Support is provided for as long as required, and terms and conditions are flexible to suit employers' and employees' needs. Support varies depending on the support organisation concerned.

Job Introduction Scheme

To assist people with disabilities to settle into a new job and to help with any additional training requirements, the Employment Service can pay a weekly grant of £75 to the employer. The job can be full or part time but must be expected to last for six months.

The grant is usually paid to the employer for the first six weeks of the disabled person's employment; in exceptional circumstances the period can be extended to 13 weeks.

The Job Introduction Scheme must be applied for before the employee starts the job. The Employment Service Disability Services Team decides on the availability and eligibility (see Chapter 6 for contact details).

Support services

There are many organisations that offer a variety of assistance both to people with disabilities and employers. These organisations may be local initiatives, national voluntary organisations or statutory bodies such as local authorities and the Employment Service.

As well as offering guidance with the Access to Work Scheme, Workstep (Supported Employment Programme) and the Job Introduction Scheme, support services can provide practical support in the following areas:

- the recruitment of people with disabilities
- the provision of job coaching/job support
- disability awareness issues
- organising work experience placements
- advice on adaptations/specialist equipment
- retention/redeployment of employees with disabilities.

There are many organisations that can provide this wide range of support to assist in the recruitment and retention of people with disabilities in the workplace. A list of useful contacts can be found in Chapter 6.

Employment policies and good practice

Introduction

Organisations that enter into both the spirit and the letter of the legislation will benefit from a wider pool of talent and experience. Concentrating on individuals' strengths and abilities will ensure that organisations gain from diversity in the workplace.

In this chapter we shall look at three key employment areas in which there is considerable scope to introduce and develop good practice:

1 recruitment and selection
2 retention and redeployment
3 work experience placements.

Many employers have displayed their commitment to good practice regarding the employment of people with disabilities by adopting the 'Positive about Disability' symbol (also known as the 'Double Tick' – ✓ ✓). This is awarded by the Employment Service to employers who demonstrate their commitment to five key areas:

1 to interview all applicants with a disability who meet the minimum criteria for a job vacancy and consider them on their abilities (guaranteed job interview scheme)

2 to ask disabled employees at least once a year what can be done to make sure they can develop and use their abilities at work

3 to make every effort to ensure that when employees become disabled they stay in employment

4 to take action to ensure that key employees develop the awareness of disability needed to make the commitments work

5 each year to review these commitments and what has been achieved, plan ways to improve on them and let all employees know about progress and future plans.

Recruitment and selection

The following recruitment process and good practice constitute the basis of an acceptable guaranteed job interview scheme (see above). This will help achieve the aim of ensuring equality of opportunity in employment and, in particular, increase the quality and quantity of employment opportunities available to people with disabilities.

Job description

The job description should be prepared and updated accurately to reflect the nature of the job. This should ensure that, if a person with a disability applies, an employer will be aware of areas where changes to existing working practices or the working environment (perhaps with equipment adaptations) are possible.

Person specification

The person specification must clearly reflect the requirements of the job and ensure that no requirements are included that would unnecessarily place a disabled applicant at a substantial disadvantage in comparison with an applicant who is not disabled.

A person specification should be prepared and used throughout the recruitment and selection process. It must clearly outline the essential skills, experience and other personal attributes necessary for any individual to carry out the duties of the job. In addition, it should detail any other skills, experience and personal attributes that may be regarded as desirable for any individual to possess in order to carry out the duties of the job.

Care must be taken to avoid the inclusion of unnecessary or marginal requirements that may lead to discrimination. Employers should also consider whether they need to stipulate that the employee must be physically fit, which could unjustifiably exclude people with certain disabilities. For example, rather than say it is necessary to have a driving licence, it may be sufficient to require an ability to travel.

Recruitment advertisements

These should give brief details of the job content as well as key essential and desirable selection criteria stated in the person specification.

All recruitment advertisements should portray a positive image and encourage applications from people with disabilities. Employers who have been awarded the Employment Service's 'Positive about Disabled People' symbol should display it prominently.

Consideration should be given to advertising in publications aimed at people with disabilities and to notifying local and national disability organisations of all vacancies.

Application form

The application form should encourage applicants to declare a disability and should explain the employer's commitment to a positive approach towards equality of opportunity in employment. The employer may also ask whether the applicant may require an adjustment in order to do the job, and what that adjustment might be.

The application form should be available in different formats, including audio, Braille, large print and electronic.

Care should be taken to avoid forms with small print and inadequate space for replies. In addition, there should be no insistence on hand-written replies.

Shortlisting

Using the person specification will readily highlight whether any applicant applying under a guaranteed job interview scheme meets all of the essential selection criteria. If so, that applicant must be granted an interview.

There may be genuine reservations about shortlisting a disabled applicant because of worries about his or her ability to fulfil the demands of the job. If so, an employer may wish to contact the applicant for more specific information. In this case the reason for contacting the applicant should be explained and the specific interest or concerns in relation to the job outlined. Negative assumptions should not be made and the applicant should always be given the benefit of the doubt.

References

Based on the person specification, reference request letters should ask only for information relevant to the job (ie extent of abilities, aptitudes and experience). This applies equally to all applicants, irrespective of any application under the guaranteed job interview scheme. No isolated reference to a disability itself should be made.

Interviews

Employers have a legal obligation under the DDA to ensure that arrangements for interviews do not place applicants with disabilities at a disadvantage to other applicants who are not disabled.

Accordingly it is suggested that employers insert the following paragraph in letters issued to the applicant inviting them for interview. For example:

> If you require assistance to attend this interview, eg use of a signer or interpreter, mini-loop induction facility or car parking within close proximity to the interview venue, or if your disability affects your access to or mobility within buildings, then please

23

contact [*named individual*] at the above address, who will be happy to provide you with assistance where possible.

This should be done well in advance of the interview so that there is time to make the necessary arrangements.

Interviews with disabled people should be conducted in the same way as those with able-bodied candidates. It is important to concentrate on abilities, skills and achievements rather than on disabilities.

Questions regarding disability on application forms and at selection interviews are acceptable provided that they are relevant to the job, are phrased in a suitable tone and are being asked for a valid reason.

Employers should follow a code of good practice by inviting a disabled person to reveal his or her disability through such questions as:

- What adjustments can we make?
- What skills and abilities do you possess that make you suitable for this job?
- What, if any, type of aids, adaptations or equipment would you require to help you do this job?

These questions concentrate on a person's ability to do the job. Interviewers should not be afraid to ask searching questions of all candidates, but they should be aware that there is a thin line between probing and being intrusive. Employers should ask about a disability only if it is, or may be, relevant to the person's ability to do the job.

The following questions put to candidates with disabilities at interview are examples of bad practice:

- What is your disability?
- Do you think you are really capable of doing this job?
- How would you manage if you were required to leave this building in an emergency? (*This type of information, ie about work location and essential health and safety at work issues, should be discussed prior to interview by those responsible for compiling the job specification and person specification and by any employee with health and safety responsibilities.*)
- Are you likely to be absent often?

Negative questions like these put candidates with disabilities at a disadvantage and do not allow them to present a positive and accurate picture of their capabilities. Managers are responsible for ensuring that sufficient comprehensive information is available to all candidates regarding the working environment and accessibility, as well as the job itself. If this information is readily available, candidates with disabilities will be able to identify potential areas of difficulty themselves.

Selection tests

Selection tests may discriminate unfairly against individuals or substantially disadvantage them. Employers may need to revise the tests or the way in which test results are assessed in order to take account of candidates with disabilities.

Employers should use only tests that are strictly relevant to the job, and they must be prepared to make reasonable adjustments for candidates with disabilities. Examples of reasonable adjustments to selection tests could include:

- accepting lower pass rates
- providing a personal reader/writer
- providing a signer/communicator
- allowing additional time during tests
- accessing specialised equipment, ie loop systems, Braille keyboards.

Medical examinations

Employers would probably be guilty of unlawful discrimination if they insisted without justification on medical checks for a person with a disability but not for others. The fact that a person has a disability is unlikely in itself to justify singling him or her out for a medical check, although such action may be justified on health and safety grounds. Having a disability need not adversely affect a person's general health.

Retention and redeployment

Introduction

The DDA Code of Practice issued by the Department for Education and Employment (DfEE) states that:

> An employer must not discriminate against an employee who becomes disabled, or has a disability which worsens. The issue of retention might also arise when an employee has a stable impairment but the nature of his employment changes. If as a result of the disability an employer's arrangements or a physical feature of the employer's premises place the employee at a substantial disadvantage in doing his existing job, the employer must first consider any

reasonable adjustment that would resolve the difficulty. The employer may also need to consult the disabled person at appropriate stages about what his needs are and what effect the disability might have on future employment, for example, where the employee has a progressive condition. The nature of the reasonable adjustments which an employer may have to consider will depend on the circumstances of the case.

In line with good employment practice, and to meet the requirements of the DDA, organisations would benefit from the introduction of a retention and redeployment policy.

A similar procedure to that described below was introduced by Dundee City Council in 1997, reflecting good management practice and complying with the requirements of the DDA. It outlines the steps to be taken in situations where existing employees who, as a result of an acquired disability or worsening condition, are considered by a medical adviser or an employer to be medically unfit to carry out the duties and responsibilities of their post, but who do not want their employment terminated on the grounds of ill-health and wish to be considered for any suitable employment within their current organisation.

Although this procedure has been adopted by a local authority, the key principles and components are transferable and can be adopted by most organisations. The procedure assumes that the employer has a personnel or human resource officer or department. If not, these responsibilities would be met from within the employer's existing resources.

Procedure

Stage 1

Either the employer's personnel department or the employer refers the employee to the Disability Employment Adviser (DEA) of the Employment Service's Disability Services Team (DST). The purpose of this referral is for the DEA/DST to produce a report that assesses the person's capabilities, strengths and weaknesses. It also provides guidance on physical restrictions and the type of duties to be avoided. The report may mention specific jobs or types of employment that would suit the person and may indicate whether he or she would be eligible for support under the Access to Work Scheme or Workstep (the Supported Employment Programme). There is no charge for this service, and it provides both an independent assessment and useful practical advice.

Stage 2

The medical adviser's assessment, the DST report, the employee's own comments, and informed input from the employing department and the personnel officer form the basis of a retention or redeployment action plan. The personnel department agrees the retention or redeployment action plan with the employing department, and guides and supports the department and the employee through the remainder of the process.

Stage 3

This part of the process depends on the results and findings of the previous stages. It calls for flexible and creative thinking tempered with realism. It is not possible to cover every aspect, but the following are adjustments that could be made to accommodate the retention or redeployment of an employee with a disability:

- adjustments to the premises
- allocating some of the disabled employee's duties to another person
- altering the employee's working hours
- retraining
- purchase, or modification, of equipment
- use of the Government's Access to Work or Supported Employment Programme etc.

In the first instance, the personnel department and the line manager(s) concerned jointly identify any existing or potential vacancies within the employing department that could, with any reasonable adjustments where necessary, be suitable for the retention and redeployment of the disabled employee. If this is not successful, existing and potential vacancies in other departments are also considered. All departments are expected to co-operate in ensuring that the company meets its obligations to employees who are disabled.

Stage 4

If there is uncertainty as to whether or not the employee could perform certain duties in a particular post, further advice is sought from the medical adviser. Where appropriate, the personnel department tries to arrange a short-term work experience placement for the employee in the relevant field of work, either in his or her own or in another department. The placement could be full-time or part-time, and the trial period normally lasts up to four weeks. Subject to medical advice, work experience placements are either unpaid, the employee remaining off sick from his or her normal duties and continuing to receive the appropriate sickness entitlements, or paid at the employee's normal rate or salary if he or she is signed off as medically fit to return to work in the temporary duties.

Stage 5

If all efforts and possibilities are unsuccessful, the position is reviewed with all parties concerned and the possibility of ill-health early retirement considered.

The procedure adopted by Dundee City Council illustrates the important stages in a policy aimed at retaining or redeploying an employee who, because of the onset or deterioration of a disability, is otherwise unable to continue in his or her current post.

Whatever policy is adopted by an employer, the employee must be consulted at all stages in the process. Assessments and reports by medical advisors, line managers and the personnel department should be compiled in agreement with the employee.

An employer operating good practice will consider and develop innovative and flexible solutions to the reasonable adjustments that may be required to retain an employee with a disability.

Consideration should be given to contacting a support service, such as the Employment Disability Unit or Capability Scotland, which can provide appropriate advice and guidance towards alternative forms of support. A list of useful contacts appears in Chapter 6.

Work experience placements

It is the experience of both the Employment Disability Unit and Capability Scotland that many employers are apprehensive about employing a person with a disability. The vast majority of these concerns are ill-founded and can stem from a lack of knowledge about the capabilities of people with disabilities and the types of support available.

One of the most effective methods for employers to improve their awareness of employment and disability issues and to demonstrate their commitment to a proactive approach in supporting people with disabilities is to offer work experience placements or job tasters within their organisation.

A work experience placement or job taster can take place under a number of guises. It is recommended that several key principles should be included in any policy or procedure adopted. It should last no more than eight weeks and be organised in such a manner that people undertaking the placement will have the maximum opportunity to:

- determine their own abilities
- identify their strengths and weaknesses
- develop new skills
- improve existing skills
- identify employment/job preferences
- improve confidence
- determine stamina levels.

A work experience placement should, ideally, be arranged through a local disability support organisation. It will be able to monitor progress and use the placement to assist in the person's job search by providing an up-to-date reference and curriculum vitae.

The terms and conditions of the work experience placement should be discussed by all the parties concerned (employer, disabled person and support organisation), and such areas as restrictions, supervisor's details, hours, duties, contact details, health and safety, employer's/public liability insurance etc should be agreed and put in writing.

Although the person is participating in a placement, he or she usually remains on welfare benefits (Job Seekers Allowance, Incapacity Benefit) and it is not expected that the employer will provide any remuneration. However, it is normal for the support organisation to reimburse the disabled person with travel and meal costs and for the person undertaking the placement to be provided with a company uniform and any safety equipment or clothing.

The introduction of a structured work experience placement programme by an organisation will give an employer and the workforce the opportunity to become more 'comfortable' with the principle of disabled people in the workplace. A placement can also benefit the company by offering them an invaluable insight into how they could improve their practice in relation to any disabled customers or shareholders.

Employers who are interested in offering work experience placements or tasters can discuss the possibility in more depth with a range of agencies such as the Employment Service and disability organisations involved in employment opportunities. The key places to advertise interest as an employer in work placements are:

- local authorities
- day centres for disabled people
- rehabilitation providers
- employment services
- local training providers
- disability organisations
- schools and colleges.

Disability etiquette

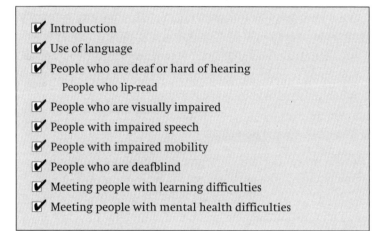

Introduction

Extensive research has shown that people with disabilities make good employees, but very often they enjoy fewer opportunities for employment because of false assumptions made by employers about disability. Yet it is sometimes the simplest things, like the words and phrases used, that can help change the way people think about and act towards disabled people.

Many of these words and phrases have been considered inappropriate for many years, and yet most people want to use language that describes disability accurately and does

35

not offend, so in this chapter we have pulled together common phrases and courtesies that aim to widen understanding of disabled people's views and preferences. These explanations are intended to be helpful, but there are no hard and fast rules. Language evolves, and sometimes words can become derogatory or take on different connotations quite quickly. As a result, often the best way to make a disabled person comfortable with you is to ask his or her advice.

We hope that the information in this chapter, approved by disabled people using Capability Scotland's services, will help with interviewing and recruiting disabled people. (Employers should bear in mind that a person may have more than one disability.)

Use of language

There is some debate amongst disabled people about the terms that should be used. The two most common terms, *disabled people* (the term recommended by the British Council of Organisations of Disabled People) and *people with disabilities*, are used in this book.

The term *the disabled* is disliked because it implies that disabled people are a group separate from everyone else. Words such as *spastic*, *cripple* and *retard* are also insulting and usually inaccurate. Many people dislike being described as a condition, for example as an *epileptic*.

Other negative phrases include the terms *suffering from* and *victim of*, which invite pity. It is a common misconception that, if a person is disabled, he or she is ill. In reality, disabled people, just like the rest of the population, vary widely in their level of general health.

The table on page 37 outlines preferences for language used by disabled people themselves.

We don't like . . .	We prefer . . .	Alternative
the disabled invalid abnormal	disabled people	people with disabilities
handicapped	disabled	has a disability
cerebral palsy sufferer	person with cerebral palsy	person who has cerebral palsy
victim of spina bifida	person with spina bifida	person who has spina bifida
wheelchair victim wheelchair-bound	wheelchair user	person who uses a wheelchair
spastic	person with cerebral palsy	person who has cerebral palsy
cripple	disabled person	person with a disability
mongol	Down's syndrome	—
mental handicap retard backward	someone with learning disabilities	someone who has a learning disability
mental illness	mental health problems	—
the blind	blind/partially sighted/visually impaired people	—
the deaf	deaf people/people with hearing impairments	—

People who are deaf or hard of hearing

People who have had a hearing impairment since birth are normally described as deaf. However, people whose hearing impairment has developed since birth are usually described as hard of hearing. The first language of people who are deaf is normally British Sign Language.

Here are a few general pointers to bear in mind when meeting someone who has experienced hearing loss:

- Remember to speak to the person you are meeting, rather than his or her interpreter.
- If you need to catch the person's attention, you should do so by (eg) lightly touching his or her shoulder or by waving your hand
- Interpreting can be tiring, so it is helpful either to offer interpreters a break or, for large meetings, to have more than one interpreter during a long or particularly fast conversation.

People who lip-read

Lip-reading is a specialist skill that some deaf people use. You can ask people if they lip-read when you meet them. If they do, it is best to:

- look directly at them and speak slowly and clearly, making sure that your face can be seen
- keep sentences reasonably short
- use suitable facial expressions or other body language to emphasise what you are trying to convey.

When arranging to meet someone who is deaf or hard of hearing, consider also:

- providing alternative arrangements if your building entry system relies on voice transfer (you could, for example, have a member of staff answer the door in person at the agreed appointment time); there are also alternatives to buzzing entry systems available that companies should consider if upgrading their systems or looking at building new premises
- setting up a meeting room free from background noise or with a minimum of noise
- fitting an induction loop, which amplifies sound for people wearing hearing aids; these are available for hire for an interview or other type of meeting or event where you know someone with a hearing aid will be present
- making clear at the outset of a meeting that one person at a time should speak and that all comments or questions should be directed through the chair.

People who are visually impaired

When meeting someone who is visually impaired it is good practice to:

- identify yourself clearly and introduce anyone else who is present in the room and indicate where they are placed in relation to the person who is visually impaired

- say the name of the person you are talking to when part of a group
- make sure you let the person know when you have ended a conversation and want to move away
- take care not to distract the guide dogs that some people have for assistance.

When arranging to meet someone with a visual impairment, ensure that:

- the room has good levels of light and a means of controlling glare
- the meeting or interview room is clearly signposted or that a member of staff is on hand to offer assistance.

People with impaired speech

As a result of their disability some people may have impaired speech. Some people also use communication aids such as alphatalkers, which are basically computers programmed to speak.

When meeting someone with a speech impairment, it is helpful to:

- be attentive and patient, because it can take longer for someone to make their point
- avoid correcting or speaking for the person; wait quietly while the person speaks and resist the temptation to finish his or her sentences
- tell the person what you don't understand and repeat what you do (if you have difficulty understanding, don't pretend!).

People with impaired mobility

When meeting someone with an impaired mobility:

- stand in front of the person and try and place yourself at his or her eye level
- do not move about so that the person has continually to change position in order to speak directly to you
- talk directly to a wheelchair user, not to his or her companion
- do not lean on a wheelchair – you are invading the body-space of the user.

There are a number of steps that businesses can take in advance if they are going to be interviewing or meeting someone who has a mobility difficulty. For example you can:

- check that there are suitable parking facilities close to your meeting place
- make sure that the entrance is level or has a ramp
- ensure that the doors are easy to open or that a member of staff is available to offer assistance with heavy or revolving doors
- check where the nearest accessible toilets are located
- organise a meeting room that is easy to get to for someone using a wheelchair or walking aids, and ensure that it has sufficient space to allow the disabled person to remain fully mobile and unobstructed.

People who are deafblind

Someone who is deafblind has an impairment affecting both sight and hearing. This makes it difficult to communicate, so many deafblind people are supported by a communicator-guide, interpreter or enabler. It is worth remembering that a deafblind person may speak to you but not hear your voice, and that some deafblind people may hear speech when there is no background noise. It is helpful to make the recommended adjustments for people with a hearing impairment and a visual impairment. The person's interpreter will support your conversation; however, you should still direct your conversation to the individual.

Meeting people with learning difficulties

The best advice is to be patient and encourage the individual. It is also worth noting the following:

- Be prepared to explain more than once if necessary, and assume you will be understood; ask the person to stop you if he or she does not understand.
- A person with a learning difficulty may have access to a job coach, advocate or support worker who provides employment assistance if required.

Meeting people with mental health difficulties

Having a mental health difficulty is not the same as having a learning difficulty. An estimated one in four people experience some kind of mental health problem in their lives. The main hurdle that people with mental health difficulties face is other people's attitudes. However, for some there may be physical barriers too, so do not assume that access will not be a problem. It is worth remembering that:

- it can be helpful to consider where the person wants to meet, because this gives him or her a choice of what would be the most comfortable setting
- sometimes people like to have the opportunity to have a friend or advocate with them
- you should not hurry people into making a decision – give them time to make up their minds.

Access and adjustments to premises

Introduction

As mentioned at the beginning of this book, employers must make reasonable adjustments to their workplace environment to ensure that disabled employees are not discriminated against; this includes, of course, physical features.

Since October 1999 all businesses, regardless of size, have had a duty (Part III of the DDA) to their customers to make reasonable adjustments to the way in which services are provided. This means that businesses already have a responsibility to look at access and make any reasonable adjustments to premises so that they do not disadvantage any existing or potential disabled customers. This includes changing policies, practices and procedures and providing auxiliary aids and adaptations such as temporary ramps.

At present, if your premises are physically difficult or impossible for people with disabilities to access, then you must provide the service by another means: you don't have to make structural changes.

However, there is a requirement under the DDA to make physical changes to premises by 2004 (Part IV of the DDA). It is sensible now for service providers to start building specifications for access improvements into refurbishment contracts or any new buildings that are planned.

If you are considering making adjustments to your premises it is worthwhile contacting the Health and Safety Executive (HSE) for advice. A number of disability organisations also offer advice and support. In this chapter we outline some basic advice to improve the accessibility of the workplace environment for someone with a disability. However, we would recommend professional help in tackling major adjustments to premises.

There are many issues to consider. For our purposes we have concentrated on parking and access, reception, moving around inside the building and toilets. Each of these areas is discussed with reference to different impairments.

Training: an issue for all staff

Employers are vicariously liable for the actions of their staff towards other employees and customers with a disability. It is both best practice and prudent to address how you deal with disabled employees or customers through a well-planned programme of disability equality or awareness training. Such training outlines the requirements of the law and practical ways in which people can support each other. Many courses also focus on disability etiquette. This can not only inform your employees but also demonstrate that you take your responsibilities under the DDA seriously. Many local and national disability organisations, including Capability Scotland, provide various types of disability equality training.

People with impaired mobility

Parking and access

The dimensions of a typical wheelchair are 60cm wide (70cm for large, powered wheelchairs and 40cm for a folded wheelchair) and 110cm long.

Good access for disabled employees (and customers) requires planning well before they reach the main entrance to the building. With foresight, problems such as uneven surfaces, kerbs and poor or limited parking facilities can be minimised or eliminated. Employers can significantly help with some of these problems, which can be potentially hazardous for *all* employees.

Car parks, if the business has them, should be level and firm. In the autumn and winter it is important to keep the car park clear of leaves, snow or ice. For safety and security, the car park should be well lit, and there should be designated disabled parking spaces, close to the entrance, with good clear access from both sides of the car door. The recommended width for a designated parking space is 3.6m; this means that three standard parking spaces can normally be turned into two designated spaces.

It is good practice, if cost allows, to have a lightweight canopy over the designated spaces, because inclement weather can make getting from a car to a wheelchair both difficult and unpleasant.

The pathway from the car park should be even, with no steps or barriers, and should be made of even, non-slip material. The ideal width for a path is at least 1.8m.

It is good practice to have one entrance for all employees. However, if the building is not accessible at the front, then good, clear signage (for example black writing on a yellow background) is required, giving details of the location of the accessible entrance. The signage should also be placed in the car park at the start of the pathway if disabled employees or customers are meant to take an alternative route.

If the main entrance for everyone has steps, a ramp is required. It is best to seek professional help in getting one built that takes into account the proper gradient needed and the amount of space available to run it up to the entrance. The ramp should have sturdy uprights and a solidly attached double handrail and kerbs on both sides, to prevent wheelchair wheels from going off course. If kerbs are not possible, a very low guard-rail can serve the same purpose. The surface of the ramp and steps should be slip-resistant and kept in good condition at all times. Again, adequate lighting and signage are required.

For small businesses, one option is a portable ramp with two tracks. These are available from specialist suppliers. Another option, if a ramp cannot be used, is to place a buzzer at the bottom of the steps, which would inform reception staff that someone was waiting and needed help. The buzzer button should be approximately 1m from the ground.

Automatic doors are ideal but, because they are not always affordable, you should try to make sure that manually opened doors are not too heavy to be opened easily. Adequate signage and handles are once more required.

Thresholds can also present problems, and ideally should be no higher than 1.5cm. The clear opening width of a door should be no less than 80cm. A frequently used door should have a kick place (40cm in depth) at the bottom to stop the footrests of a wheelchair from causing damage. The footrests can also help open the door. It also helps if a door has a vision panel no higher than 90cm from the floor so that people, including other wheelchair users, can see through to the other side. Finally, all hinged doors should open wide enough to allow sufficient room for a wheelchair user to get through.

For smaller employers, an economical way of eliminating a threshold is to put a bevelled piece of wood on either side. Where space is very restricted, changing the direction in which the door opens may be another way of making use of the full width of the door opening.

Reception

All employees and visitors benefit from an obstruction-free, well-lit reception area. Handrails are useful in larger receptions to aid people with mobility problems. However, it is even more important to have a solid non-slip floor which is on one level.

Frequently receptions are built without any recognition of the fact that people at wheelchair height cannot be seen. Where possible, it is good practice to provide a lowered section of the counter. If this is not practicable, then the receptionist can be made aware of the need to come out from behind the desk to greet any visitors using a wheelchair. One of the big differences any company can make, regardless of its size, is to train its front-of-house staff to deal with disabled people in a reasonable, non-discriminatory way.

Inside the building

Many of the usual rules about even surfaces and non-slip flooring apply throughout buildings.

For people with impaired mobility, the corridors should be at least 0.9m wide to allow the passage of a wheelchair and other users. The corridor has to be at least 1.2m wide to enable a wheelchair user to turn. A very long corridor could have a rest area with somewhere to sit, to make it easier for people with mobility difficulties to pause.

Doors opening onto corridors can also cause obstructions. Often all that is required is to hinge or hang them so that they open inwards. Lift access should also be wide enough to accommodate a wheelchair; the control buttons are best placed no higher than 1.2m from the floor.

Toilets

It is appropriate to have a unisex toilet for people with disabilities or to make all toilets fully accessible.

The door on the toilet should open outwards and be at least 90cm wide. Because the wheelchair user must be able to turn the wheelchair and close the door once they have entered the cubicle, a space of 1.5m is required inside. In case of emergency, it must be possible to open the door from the outside.

It is good practice to look also at the space required to get to the toilet seat. Room on both sides means that people can transfer over from either direction. Support rails and vertical grab rails should also be installed to help with such movements. The middle of the toilet itself should be about 50cm away from the wall with the grab rail. The toilet seat should be raised to the same height as the seat of a wheelchair, ie 45–50cm.

The mirror, hand dryer, towel dispenser and toilet roll holder should be situated no higher than 90cm above the floor to ensure they are all placed low enough for a wheelchair user to use. Lever-type taps are preferred, because they are easier to turn on and off.

Wheelchair users should be able to get to the front of the washbasin easily. The edge of the washbasin should be 75 to 80cm above floor level. The surround should be not more than 50cm deep. Clearance of 65 to 70cm is needed under the washbasin.

People with a visual impairment

Parking and access

Signage for both the car park and entrance should be clear and give straightforward instructions on how to enter the building. Black letters on a white or yellow background in a large, sans serif font is best. In the car park there should be good lighting and designated parking spaces as close as possible to the main entrance.

Visually impaired people detect that they are at the

bottom of a staircase when their stick hits the first step. At the top of a staircase, however, a tactile strip can warn them that an obstacle is near.

The main entrance to the building should also be obvious. This can be done by making it a different colour from the rest of the walkway and the handles a different colour from the door. To prevent people with impaired vision from bumping into a glass door, it should be marked with an easily distinguished strip or design half way up.

Reception

For people with a visual impairment the reception should have adequate lighting, signage and colour contrasts. Although it is best to avoid sudden changes in level, it is possible to give warnings of low ceilings and other changes through the level of lighting and through colour or texture. Where a building has glass doors, it is best to use non-reflective glass.

Again, well-trained reception staff can make a huge difference in helping someone with a visual impairment to get about in a building. Information should also be provided in a range of formats (eg large print, audio).

Inside the building

Clear direction signs are useful for all staff who need to find their way around and, in larger buildings, a groundfloor map is also useful. Any map or sign provided can be made tactile, which will help people with a visual impairment. Other signs should be made using non-shiny material, contrasting lettering (eg yellow on black) and good direct lighting so that they are clear. Signage should also be in upper and lower case lettering not less than 2cm high.

The floor should also be non-slip and even. Mats with tapered edges will minimise risks to most users. All corridors should be well lit and as free from obstacles as possible. It is also best if doors are hinged to open from the main corridor inwards; if possible, they should have a vision panel which allows people to see into other corridors.

If there is a lift in the building for visitors to get from one floor to another, it should be marked with a pictogram (white on a coloured background). Numbers and symbols on the buttons should be raised or etched and easily identifiable by a visually impaired person. Where possible, both a floor announcer and a visual signal should announce the arrival of the lift and of floors reached.

Where there are stairs, the staircase should have a sturdy handrail. It is also helpful if the colour both of the risers and of a slip-resistant strip across each tread contrasts with the main colour of the step. This helps visually impaired people judge the height of steps. Risers should be no more than 15cm high. Treads should be no less than 28cm deep. A wider strip of a contrasting colour at the top and bottom of the staircase will indicate to people with impaired vision that a staircase is near.

Toilets

It is appropriate to have a unisex toilet for people with disabilities or to make all toilets fully accessible. Colour contrast between fittings and walls is helpful to people with visual impairment.

People with a hearing impairment

Parking and access

For hearing-impaired people, an entry-phone system with a visual 'enter' indicator can be installed. Again, clear signage and directions to the main entrance are also useful.

Reception

It is important to provide a clear reception area that allows anyone who uses sign language or lip-reading to see the receptionist clearly when he or she speaks. Different types of equipment, such as a device for amplifying the receptionist's voice and an induction loop for someone with a hearing aid, are also useful. Furthermore, information should be provided in a range of formats (eg print, text telephones).

Useful contacts

Angus Council
Employment Disability Unit
Personnel Department
County Buildings
Market Street
Forfar
DD8 3LG

Tel: 01307 461460

Association for Supported Employment Agencies – Wales
89 Talbot Road
Talbot Green
Pontyclun
R C T
CF72 8AE

Tel: 01443 226664

British Deaf Association
1–3 Worship Street
London
EC2A 2AB

Tel: 020 7588 3520

British Epilepsy Association
New Anstey House
Gateway Drive
Yeadon
Leeds
LS19 7XY

Tel: 0113 2108800

Capability Scotland
Employment Development Department
7a Loaning Road
Edinburgh
EH7 6JE

Tel: 0131 6614735

Chartered Institute of Personnel and Development
CIPD House
Camp Road
Wimbledon
London
SW19 4UX

Tel: 020 8971 9000

Disability Action
Portside Business Park
189 Airport Road West
Belfast
BT3 9ED

Tel: 02890 297880

Disability Rights Commission
2nd Floor
Arndale House
The Arndale Centre
Manchester
M4 3AQ

Tel: 0161 2611700

Disability Rights Commission
1st Floor
Riverside House
502 Gorgie Road
Edinburgh
EH11 4AF

Tel: 0131 4444300

Disability Rights Commission
6 Ty-Nant Court
Ty-Nant Road
Morganstown
Cardiff
CF15 8LW

Tel: 02920 815600

Disability Rights Commission Helpline
Freepost MID02164
Stratford-upon-Avon
CV37 9BR

Tel: 0845 7622633

Disability Wales/Anabledd Cymru
Wernddu Court
Caerphilly Business Park
Van Road
Caerphilly
CF83 3ED

Tel: 02920 887325

Dumfries and Galloway Council
Hope Service
17 Buccleuch Street
Dumfries
DG1 2AT

Tel: 01387 249172

Dundee City Council
Employment Disability Unit
Dunsinane Avenue
Dundee
DD2 3QN

Tel: 01382 828180

Dyslexia Institute
133 Gresham Road
Staines
Middlesex
TW18 2AJ

Tel: 01784 463851

**Employer's Forum on Disability –
Northern Ireland**
Banbridge Enterprise Centre
Scarva Road Industrial Estate
Banbridge
BT32 3QD

Tel: 028 40624526

**Employment Service
Disability Service Team**
3rd Floor
Wallace House
Maxwell Place
Stirling
FK8 1JU

Tel: 01786 424233

Employment Service
Disability Service Team
4th Floor
Newcroft House
Market Street East
Newcastle
NE1 6ND

Tel: 0191 2208988

Employment Service
Disability Service Team
5th Floor
24–26 Torphichen Street
Edinburgh
EH3 8JP

Tel: 0131 4565200

Employment Service
Disability Service Team
21 Herschell Street
Anniesland
Glasgow
G13 1HR

Tel: 0141 8002200

Employment Service
Disability Service Team
4th Floor
Metropolitan House
31–33 High Street
Inverness
IV1 1JD

Tel: 01463 888280

Employment Service
Disability Service Team
17 Grange Street
Kilmarnock
KA1 2DF

Tel: 01563 505850

Employment Service
Disability Service Team
132 Seagate
Dundee
DD1 2HB

Tel: 01382 373400

Employment Service
Disability Service Team
1st Floor
2 Duchess Place
Hadley Road
Birmingham
B16 8NS

Tel: 0121 4525332

Employment Service
Disability Service Team
Pepper Road
Hunslet
Leeds
LS10 2NP

Tel: 0113 2710333

Employment Service
Disability Service Team
4th Floor
Caradog House
1–6 St Andrews Place
Cardiff
CF10 3SE

Tel: 02920 423070

**Employment Service
Disability Service Team**
Adelaide House
39–49 Adelaide Street
Belfast
BT2 8FD

Tel: 02890 257472

**Employment Service
Disability Service Team**
Newtown House
Maid Marion Way
Nottingham
NG1 6GG

Tel: 0115 9895850

**Employment Service
Disability Service Team**
Level 1
236 Grays Inn Road
London
WC1X 8HL

Tel: 020 7211 4585

Employment Service
Disability Service Team
Unit 19
Eagleswood Business Park
Woodlands Lane
Bradley Stoke
Bristol
BS32 4EU

Tel: 01454 848551

Enable Services
The Adelphi Centre
12 Commercial Road
Glasgow
G5 0PQ

Tel: 0141 4297895

Epilepsy Association of Scotland
48 Govan Road
Glasgow
G51 1JL

Tel: 0141 427 4911

The Equality Commission for Northern Ireland
Disability Unit
Glendinning House
Murray Street
Belfast
BT1 6DP

Tel: 02890 500600

Hansel Alliance
Hansel Village
Symington
Ayrshire
KA1 5PU

Tel: 01563 830340

**Headway National Head Injuries
Association Limited**
4 King Edward Court
King Edward Street
Nottingham
NG1 1EW

Tel: 0115 9240800

Highland Council
Social Work Services
Carsegate House
Glendoe Terrace
Inverness
IV3 6ED

Tel: 01463 724024

ME Association
4 Corringham Road
Stanford-le-Hope
Essex
SS17 0AH

Tel: 01375 642466

MENCAP
MENCAP National Centre
123 Golden Lane
London
EC1Y 0RT

Tel: 020 7454 0454

National Autistic Society
Central Chambers
109 Hope Street
Glasgow
G2 6LL

Tel: 0141 2218090

National Schizophrenia Fellowship (NSF)
28 Castle Street
Kingston-upon-Thames
Surrey
KT1 1SS

Tel: 020 8547 3937

National Society for Epilepsy
Chescham Lane
Chalfont St Peter
Buckinghamshire
SL9 0RJ

Tel: 01494 601300

Northern Ireland Union of Supported Employment
58 Strand Road
Derry
BT48 7AJ

Tel: 02871 377709

Perth and Kinross Council
Employment Disability Unit
6 Rose Terrace
Perth
PH1 5HA

Tel: 01738 442314

Quest Supported Employment Agency
435 Cowbridge Road East
Canton
Cardiff
CF5 1JH

Tel: 02920 373305

Royal Association for Disability and Rehabilitation (RADAR)
12 City Forum
250 City Road
London
EC1V 8AF

Tel: 020 7250 3222

Royal National Institute for the Blind (RNIB)
224 Great Portland Street
London
W1W 5AA

Tel: 020 7388 1266

Saville & Holdsworth (UK) Limited
The Pavillion
1 Atwell Place
Surrey
KT7 0NA

Tel: 020 8398 4170

Scope
6 Market Road
London
N7 9PW

Tel: 020 7619 7100

Scottish Association of Mental Health
Cumbrae House
15 Carlton Court
Glasgow
G5 9JP

Tel: 0141 568 7000

Scottish Union of Supported Employment
32 Redhall Crescent
Edinburgh
EH14 2NU

Tel: 0131 5394967

Ulster Supported Employment Ltd
88–136 Lawnbrook Avenue
Belfast
BT13 2QD

Tel: 02890 322881

With over 100,000 members, the **Chartered Institute of Personnel and Development** is the largest organisation in Europe dealing with the management and development of people. The CIPD operates its own publishing unit, producing books and research reports for human resource practitioners, students, and general managers charged with people management responsibilities.

Currently there are over 150 titles, covering the full range of personnel and development issues. The books have been commissioned from leading experts in the field and are packed with the latest information and guidance to best practice.

For free copies of the CIPD Books Catalogue, please contact the publishing department:
Tel: 020 8263 3387
Fax: 020 8263 3850
E-mail: *publish@cipd.co.uk*
Web: *www.cipd.co.uk*

Orders for books should be sent direct to:
Plymbridge Distributors
Estover
Plymouth
Devon PL6 7PY
Tel: +44 (0) 1752 202301
Fax: +44 (0) 1752 202333
E-mail: orders@plymbridge.com

Bullying and Sexual Harassment

by

Tina Stephens

Most organisations are aware of the serious legal implications of allowing bullying or sexual harassment to flourish in the workplace. Morale can be affected if management does not act, with consequences for productivity and effectiveness. Up to date and to the point, this guide will show how to:

- write, establish and develop a formal policy for dealing with both bullying and sexual harassment
- understand and communicate the influence of bullying and harassment on absenteeism, productivity and reputation
- establish formal and informal complaints procedures
- train managers to recognise problems early and raise awareness.

1999   96 pages   ISBN 0 85292 825 4   **£9.99**

Career Development

by

Tricia Jackson

How do HR practitioners manage and develop the careers of their staff in today's fast-moving and rapidly changing world of work? What is a career, when employees change jobs more frequently than ever before and the concept of 'the job for life' has apparently withered and died? This Good Practice guide will help the reader understand and use the competencies required for good career development, including negotiation and communication, and coaching and performance appraisal.

2000   112 pages   ISBN 0 85292 851 3   **£9.99**

Creating a Staff Handbook

by

Clare Hogg

The staff handbook is the organisation's bible. It is the first place employees will look for essential information on the practices and procedures of their workplace. How do you make sure the staff handbook is the definitive source of information it should be? This invaluable guide shows:

- how to produce, maintain and revise a staff handbook
- examples from staff handbooks
- the legal aspects and communication issues.

1999   112 pages   ISBN 0 85292 822 X   **£9.99**

Drugs and Alcohol Policies

by

Tricia Jackson

This guide shows how to put alcohol and drugs policies into practice and how to make them really work. *Drugs and Alcohol Policies*:

- provides help on how to write alcohol and drugs policies
- considers the health and safety aspects of alcohol and drug abuse
- tackles related problems such as absenteeism, competence and relationships at work
- explains employers' rights and obligations under UK law.

1999   112 pages   ISBN 0 85292 811 4   **£9.99**

Handling Grievances

by

Tricia Jackson

This book provides the essential tools and techniques for handling grievances. It explains in detail how to:

- introduce (or enhance) a comprehensive grievance procedure
- avoid damaging disputes and unnecessary legal claims
- conduct a professional grievance interview
- respond effectively to employee worries and complaints.

2000   104 pages   ISBN 0 85292 885 8   **£9.99**

Induction

by

Alan Fowler

It is easy to forget how difficult it is to start a new job: the new colleagues, the sense of anti-climax, and the inscrutable work practices. This guide covers:

- why induction is important
- the first day at work and what the new starter must know
- a checklist of induction tasks
- how to widen the new starter's knowledge over the first month.

1999   96 pages   ISBN 0 85292 814 9   **£9.99**

Internet and E-Mail Use and Abuse

by

Clare Hogg

Clare Hogg explores the huge scope of new electronic communications, pitfalls to avoid and ways of maximising their
potential. Clear, thorough and fully up to date, this book
offers definitive practical advice on:

- stamping out misuse (bullying, libel, breaches of
  privacy, offensive material and unfocused
  browsing)
- advertising vacancies and attracting applicants
  through electronic media
- striking the right balance between impersonal
  e-memos, meetings and other face-to-face methods
  of human contact.

2000   96 pages   ISBN 0 85292 881 5   **£9.99**

Rewarding Teams

by

Michael Armstrong

How do you reward your staff to ensure their best performance as a team? Fitting a reward strategy to your team and
balancing financial and non-financial incentives are just
two of the many issues to consider. Reward expert Michael
Armstrong brings you the very latest thinking on these
issues, with case studies and examples of how top organisations solve the dilemma of motivation and reward.

Practical and definitive, this guide covers:

- how to develop team pay
- the pros and cons of team pay
- how to manage team reward processes
- bonus formulae and their performance criteria.

The steps to effective implementation set out a Team
Reward Action Plan that will help you create a scheme that
benefits all.

2000   112 pages   ISBN 0 85292 860 2   **£9.99**

Part-time Workers

by

Anna Allan and Lucy Daniels

According to recent government figures, a quarter of the UK workforce works part-time. But how is part-time working defined, and what effect will the Part-time Workers Directive have?

This guide includes:

- definitions of annual hours and zero hours contracts and how to decide which is best for your organisation
- the benefits of employing part-timers – and the practical considerations
- how managing part-timers differs to managing full-timers – and how it is exactly the same
- strategies for including part-time workers
- monitoring the performance of part-time workers – and what you can expect from them.

The guide explains the differences between job-sharing and job-splitting, flexible part-time working and term-time working, detailing the issues of each for organisations.

1999   104 pages   ISBN 0 85292 813 0   **£9.99**

Smoking Policies

by

Tricia Jackson

Smoking-free environments are becoming the norm in the workplace. But how can organisations enforce them in a way that is both effective and fair? This guide:

- explains the reasons for introducing a smoking policy
- shows how to develop a smoking policy – and how to make sure it works
- discusses the legal and social implications
- details the best way to approach grievance and disciplinary procedures.

It will help to tackle one of the most common – and most contentious – issues in the workplace in a way that ensures everybody wins.

1999   96 pages   ISBN 0 85292 812 2   **£9.99**